A workbook guide, on How to gain an Outlook, while you Affirm and Manifest

Through Self Care, Inner Strength & Introspective Shadow Work

By: Latoria Bowie

Published by Latoria Bowie / CK Melanin LLC

ISBN 9798717461306

www.ckmelan.in

Contents

Contents

Contents

INTRODUCTION

I guess it's time to get personal, I'm Latoria but you can call me Tori. Since the onslaught of Covid, I've taken the time to get to know myself a little better and manifest the life I want.

My goal, for you, is to come to the same realization. That you can manifest the life you want, how you want it; while learning more about yourself in the process.

DEDICATION

Who this workbook is for

This Workbook is intended for the not-so average woman.

A woman who, for all intents and purposes, doesn't have a

clue.

A clue about what she's doing or where she's going.

This one's for you Girl!

*You'll notice blank drawings throughout the book. Let
your creativity shine as you color in your future.

FLUORESCENCE

A poem about blossoming

Little Seeds Of Wonder
They start out as a twinkle;
An ever fleeting thought
How often are they implanted?
Into your mind field of dreams,
Rows of everything you imagined life to be.
How often do you plant a seed?
Sewing and Reaping
Off one little dream.....
Fed and nurtured; watered and weathered;
That is, until it becomes untethered From the
drought of doubt
Growing up, as it sees fit.
Until you can hardly sit
Because watching your dreams become a
reality
Is a sight one should hardly miss

By: Latoria Bowie

OPEN FOR BUSINESS

Rise & Shine Beautiful

What time does your shop open
up?
In your hand, a nice brewed cup.
Taking a sip with your eyes shut,
Wait..... isn't that your third cup?!?

By: Latoria Bowie

SELF-CARE

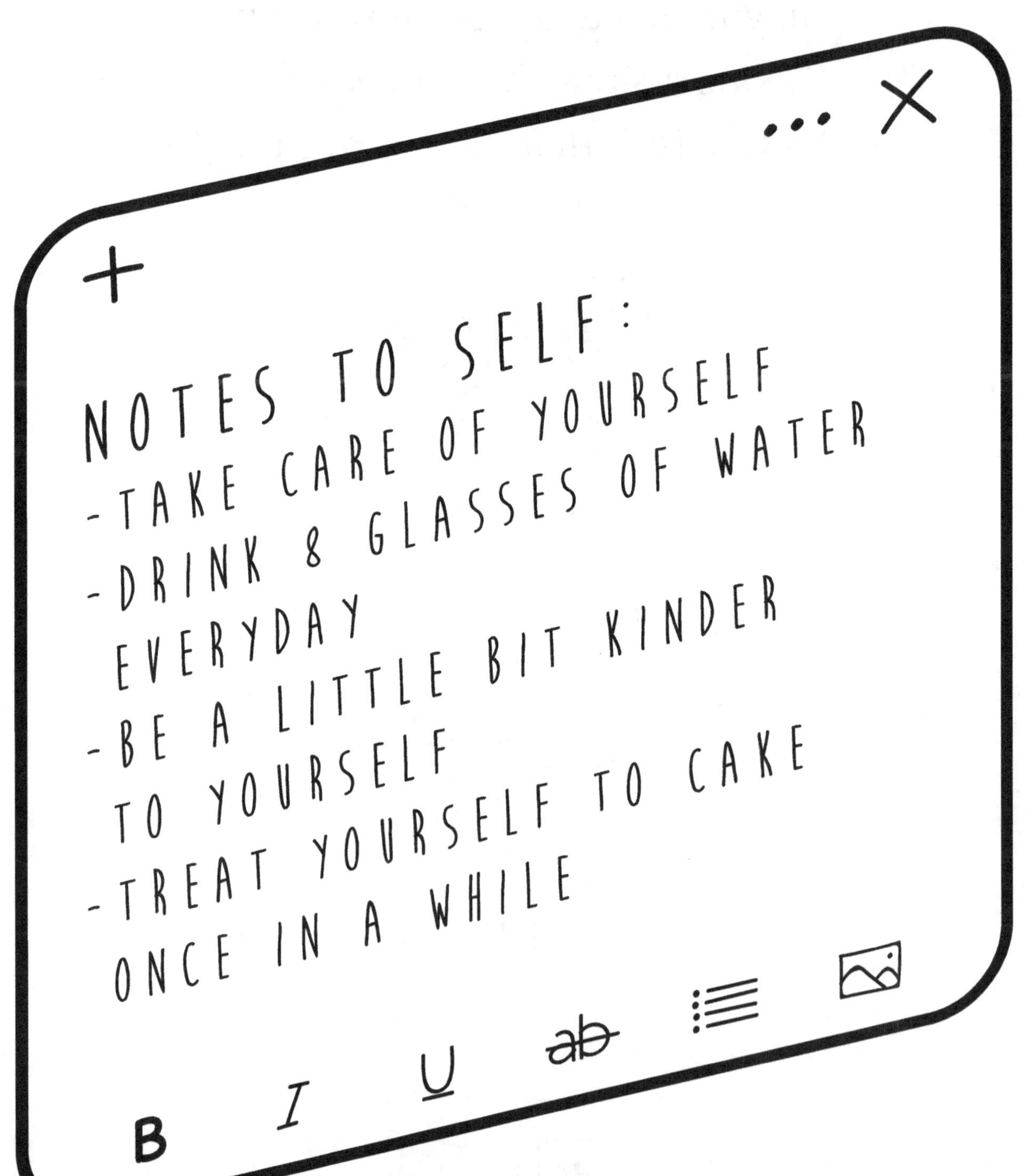

+
... ×
NOTES TO SELF:
-TAKE CARE OF YOURSELF
-DRINK 8 GLASSES OF WATER
EVERYDAY
-BE A LITTLE BIT KINDER
TO YOURSELF
-TREAT YOURSELF TO CAKE
ONCE IN A WHILE
B I U

AFFIRMATION CHALLENGE

Affirm who you are

I am divinely made for a higher purpose

I am in perfect balance, lacking nothing

I am full of peace, joy, and bliss

Break the the affirmation above into shorter

affirmations you can implement into your

vocabulary

List 6:

____

____

____

____

____

____

INNER PEACE BODY SCRUB

With Hemp Seed Oil

It is believed that up to 12 amino acids are made in the human body, but the remaining nine (known as essential amino acids) must be supplied through diet.

Hemp seed oil comes from the small seeds of the Cannabis sativa plant.

The seeds do not contain the same levels of compounds as the plant itself, but they still have a large amount of nutrients, fatty acids, and more.

Amino acids are the precursors to neurotransmitters – the natural biochemicals that facilitate communication between brain cells, controlling emotions, memory, moods, behaviour, sleep, and learning abilities.

*Hemp Seed oil, not to be confused as cannabidiol (CBD) oil, contains 21 Amino Acids.

Recipe——————————>

INNER PEACE BODY SCRUB

Recipe

3 Oz of Pink Himalayan Sea Salt

1 Oz of Collodial Oatmeal

1/2 Oz of Brown Sugar

1/2 Oz of Ground Coffee (*optional- great for cellulite)

1 Oz of Hemp Seed Oil

1 Oz of Jojoba Oil

7 Drops of Lavender Essential Oil

10 Drops of Eucalyptus Essential Oil

First, mix the dry ingredients together to remove lumps and clumps.

Next, add warmed oil blend to dry ingredients. Stirring until you get your desired consistency.

Apply the scrub with your hands or an exfoliating tool, then rinse with luke warm water.

AFFIRMATION CHALLENGE #2

No more criticizing yourself! It's time for you to rebuild your confidence by working on the areas you feel you're weak in.

I am happy, I am healthy, I am content, I am peaceful, I am prosperous, I am abundant.

I effortlessly let go of thoughts that
drain me and refocus my attention on
thoughts that empower me.

Weaknesses	Strengths

BODY OIL RECIPE

Moisturize Your Skin, Uplift your Spirits

1 fl oz of Jojoba Oil

1 fl oz of GrapeSeed Oil

5 Drops of Eucalyptus Essential Oil

5 Drops of Lavender Essential Oil

5 Drops Tea Tree Essential Oil

First, heat the carrier oils in a double boiler.

*Warm some water in a microwave safe bowl,

then place GLASS of carrier oils into water

Once oils are warm, add essential oils then

blend

*Optional

Create a luxurious and aromatic body oil by adding a cup of dried flower petals to the blend!

First, place dried flower petals into air tight glass jar.

Then, add mixture of warm oils on top of your petals. Be sure to add enough of the oil the mixture to submerge the petals.

Place airtight lid on jar, then store away from direct sunlight. In cool, dark space.

Allow to steep for up to 5 days.

Strain your oil into an Amber dropper bottle, in order to preserve your blend further.

CLAY MASK RECIPE

Detox from Head to Toe

Although you may be a home body, the outside environment is
polluted by heavy metals like lead and mercury.
Bentonite Clay acts as a magnet and extracts those heavy metals,
bacteria, and sebum.

For Body:

3oz Bentonite Clay

1oz Rose Petal Powder (optional)

1/2 Oz of Jojoba Oil

1/2 Oz of Almond Oil

5 Drops of Eucalyptus Essential Oil

5 Drops of Tea Tree Essential Oil

First, slowly add water to your Bentonite
Clay; continue to stir until all of the clay
and water is mixed.
Then add your warmed oil blend.
Next, apply the clay mixture to your
Body, Face, or Hair.
You could even treat yourself and do a
complete Body Mask!
Allow the clay mask to completely dry,
for up to 20 minutes, before you rinse
with warm water.
*Optional: Add coconut or rose water to
your Bentonite Clay to rehydrate &
moisturize your skin even further!

For Hair:

3oz Bentonite Clay

1/2 Oz of Jojoba Oil

1/2 Oz of Jamaican Black Castor
Oil

5 Drops of Peppermint Essential Oil

5 Drops of Tea Tree Essential Oil

For Face:

3oz Bentonite Clay

1/2 Oz of Jojoba Oil

1/2 Oz of Sunflower Oil

5 Drops of Eucalyptus Essential Oil

5 Drops of Tea Tree Essential Oil

5 drops of Lavender Essential Oil

BATH TEA RECIPE

Relax and Unwind. You deserve it

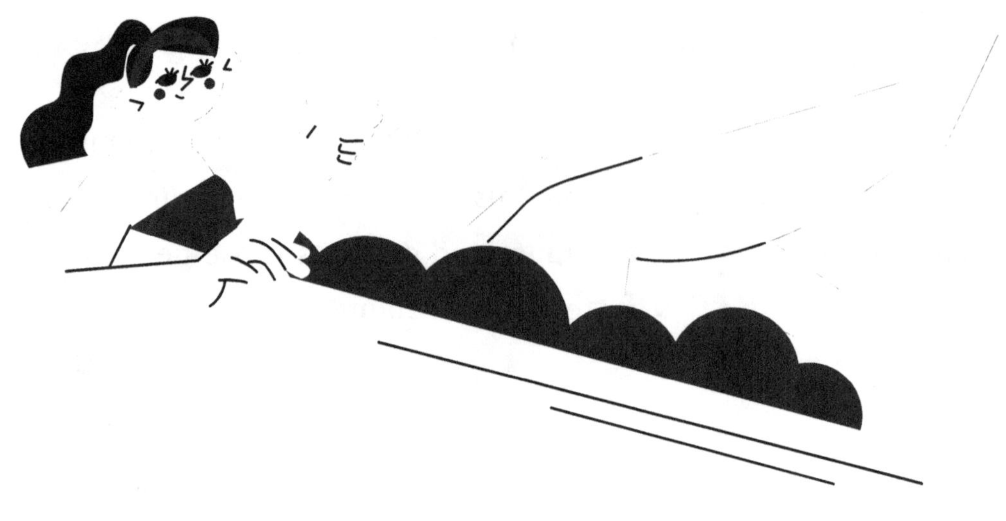

Bath Teas are made by infusing dried herbs and essential oils into your hot bath. You can also add salts and dried fruit to your tea.

Bath Tea (Brewed)
2 Cups Water
1/2 oz of Dried Rose Petals
1/2 oz of Dried Lavender Buds
1/2 oz of Dried Jasmine
5 Drops of Rosemary Essential Oil
1 Tablespoon of Jojoba Oil

Add the Jojoba Oil and Rosemary Essential Oil to your Dried Herbs then give it a stir. Pour boiling water on top of your herbs and allow to steep for 5 minutes, while your bath water runs. Strain your tea into a bowl or cup then transfer the blend into your bath. Step in and relax.

BATH TEA RECIPE

SOULFUL SOUNDS & MELODIES

Think positive thoughts while you soak, play some R&B, light a few candles, and have a glass of wine

SANGO FT SPZRKT- MIDDLE OF THINGS REMIX	3:18
SNOH AALEGRA- I WANT YOU AROUND	3:33
EMERYLD- DO IT	3:01
SEBASTIAN MIKAEL- TIME	3:31
ARIA BLEU- JOYRIDE	3:52
GUORDON BANKS- KEEP YOU IN MIND	3:16
ESTA FT SPZRKT- CANT WAIT	2:56

INNER STRENGTH

INNER STRENGTH CHALLENGE #1

I challenge you to....

Devote 1 Hour a Day to Self-Reflection

Did you rise in a good mood?
Did you learn a valuable lesson or gain more insight on a topic?
Where can this lesson be applied?
Did you remember to breathe?
Commend yourself for the goals you were able to accomplish today.

Gimme' the Scoop ⟶

INNER STRENGTH CHALLENGE #2

Let's test your manifestation skills!

I challenge you to.......

Manifest 1 thing a Day.....
For the next 5 Days

It doesn't have to be anything spectacular, just

something simple like:

Finding a closer parking spot at the grocery

store

Finding money on the ground

Extra fries in your bag

Being able to skip the line or being first at the

register Receiving Positive News

Finishing a task or accomplishing a Goal

Manifestation Tracker ⟶

MANIFESTATION TRACKER

MONDAY

TUESDAY

WEDNESDAY

THURSDAY

FRIDAY

MANIFESTATION TRACKER

MONDAY

TUESDAY

WEDNESDAY

THURSDAY

FRIDAY

MANIFESTATION TRACKER

MONDAY

TUESDAY

WEDNESDAY

THURSDAY

FRIDAY

MANIFESTATION TRACKER

MONDAY

TUESDAY

WEDNESDAY

THURSDAY

FRIDAY

MANIFESTATION TRACKER

MONDAY

TUESDAY

WEDNESDAY

THURSDAY

FRIDAY

INTROSPECTIVE SHADOW WORK

Become Familiar with your doubts, then throw them out

Shadow Work Stipulations

Stipulation 1: Be Honest & Truthful

Stipulation 2: 1 page per prompt (front & back)

Stipulation 3: Dive Deep & Feel your emotions

Prompt 1

If I could say one thing to the person who hurt me the most, what would it be and why?

Prompt 2

What was the hardest thing I've ever had to
do and how has it impacted me since?

Prompt 3

If present me could talk to myself from
10 years ago, I would say....

Prompt 4

What trauma triggers are common in my everyday life? How do I deal with them and where do I think they come from?

Prompt 5

How have I internalized my parent's
judgement?

Prompt 6

Write the words I need to hear right
now:

Prompt 7

When was the last time I witnessed self-destructive behavior in myself? Describe it and my emotions at the time:

Prompt 8

What emotions do I barely express to others and when did I start hiding these emotions?

Prompt 9

When I think of my future, I am most afraid of:

Prompt 10

What do I do that holds me back the most in life?

Prompt 11

Am I okay with the fact that not everyone will like me? Why or why not? How does this make me feel?

Prompt 12

If I could say one thing to the person who hurt me the most, what would it be and why?

Prompt 13

What emotions do I try to avoid the most? Why am I afraid of letting myself feel these emotions?

Prompt 14

How does the feeling of envy show
up in my life? Where does it come
from?

Prompt 15

What relationships and friendships do I have that are unhealthy:

Prompt 16

What do I need to forgive myself
for? Why have I struggled to
forgive myself for this?

MAID SERVICES

It's time to let go

Although easier said than done, letting go of things that don't serve you, is one of the smartest and healthiest things you could do for yourself.

I'm not saying you have to do something drastic but just start small…

Organize your Closet or
Storage Space
Declutter your purses and
emails (those types of things
can weigh you down girl!)
Donate your old clothes
Get your car Detailed
Paint your nails
Don't Trip! (Seriously girl, that
stuff hurts)
Laugh it off!

Freedom Tracker ⟶

MENTAL FREEDOM
TRACKER

I LET GO OF:

____

____

____

____

____

WHAT I LEARNED:

____

____

____

____

____

WORDS TO SELF:

____

____

DATE: _______________________

MENTAL FREEDOM
TRACKER

I LET GO OF:

____

____

____

____

____

____

WHAT I LEARNED:

____

____

____

____

____

WORDS TO SELF:

____

____

____

DATE: ________________

MENTAL FREEDOM
TRACKER

I LET GO OF:

____

____

____

____

____

____

WHAT I LEARNED:

____

____

____

____

____

____

WORDS TO SELF:

____

____

____

DATE: _______________

MENTAL FREEDOM
TRACKER

I LET GO OF:

____

____

____

____

____

____

WHAT I LEARNED:

____

____

____

____

____

WORDS TO SELF:

____

____

____

DATE: __________________

MENTAL FREEDOM
TRACKER

I LET GO OF:

____

____

____

____

____

____

WHAT I LEARNED:

____

____

____

____

____

WORDS TO SELF:

____

____

____

DATE: _______________

DECISIONS, DECISIONS

This is a safe space for your thoughts and ideas.
As the famous saying goes, "Rome wasn't built
in a day." It takes time for you to bloom. Don't
know where to go or what to do? That's fine,
we've all been there. So, just take your time.

Goals for the week:

RELEASE

A letter to your younger self

REVIVIFY

A letter to your future self

RENEW

A letter to the person of your choosing

Journal

"I allow love to fill every inch of my skin, and I will embrace
the warmth this love gives to me"

"I am worthy of accomplishment, success,
and abundance"

"I move in alignment with my highest self.
I affirm my ability to merge timelines, and rejoice as everything comes to me with ease"

"I have all the happiness, love and positive energy
I need today to have the most amazing day"

"My energy creates my reality. What I focus on is
what I will manifest"

"Peace and Happiness is my BIRTHRIGHT!"

"Peace and Happiness is my BIRTHRIGHT!"

"Energy flows where my intention goes"

CLOSING REMARKS

It's been real

Ahh, so you've made it to the end. See how easy
that was?
Doing the work to better yourself doesn't just end
here though. You have to remember to grow through
it, not just go through it.

To my readers:

*I affirm that every reader of this workbook will
become the person they've always wanted to be
and go on to accomplish great things.*

Where to find me:
Follow me on insta 
@ckmindandbody & share your journey with
me!
Don't forget to tag us & use #melanatedcare in
your post.

You can also Shop for our Ready Made,
Self-Care products
visit: www.ckmelan.in